IRISH
SONGS
of the
SEA

54 Complete Songs with Words, Music and Chords

by James N. Healy

OSSIAN

published in association
with Mercier Press

But our wind-jammers all have vanished
They're extinct forever more
They shall never again cross the harbour
As they did in days of yore.

To Des, Cha and Kevin
In memory of our wild youth
By the seashore of Ardmore
And the times I fell out of the boat.

Design by John Loesberg
Printed by Lee Press Ltd., Cork.

OSSIAN PUBLICATIONS LTD.
P.O.Box 84, Cork, Ireland
E Mail: ossian@eirenet.net
Internet: http://www.eirenet.net/ossian/

OMB 119
ISBN 1 900428 45 8

Preface

Ireland is an island, and completely dominated by the sea. The Atlantic Ocean thunders on three sides of us. Through the centuries it has eaten into our coastline, shaping it into weird and beautiful headlands. On the other side is a channel separating us from our old protagonist, Britain — the jumping off ground for many of the ancient peoples, Celts and others, who sought a home on our shores.

We too did our share of raiding on the Welsh and Cornish coasts, and it was as the result of such an excursion that St Patrick was brought to our shore. We in turn were raided and colonised by the Danes and in earlier times by forgotten sea raiders, who through the imagination of the tellers of tales became the fearsome one-eyed Fomorians of myth. It was from over the sea that the Normans came to our shore and hope of deliverance was looked to from the sea over the following centuries, mainly from the Spaniards and the French. In return the sea carried our manhood to die in Spain, or fight in France; to be transported to Van Dieman's Land, and later, following the dreadful days of a famine in the middle of the last century, to seek riches (maybe) in the Golden Land of Amerikay.

There have been songs for all these things, although considering Ireland's dependence on the sea, not as many as apply to other subjects — perhaps because many of such songs tended to be of an international, rather than a national, nature. Nevertheless there have been many, and to make for easier selection I have divided them in this revised format of my *Irish Ballads and Songs of the Sea* into sections. Some songs have been added and some taken away in this new edition. Notes are incorporated with the index which follows.

Contents

IV. SPANISH WINE AND WILD GEESE

V. COME BACK TO ERIN

VII. INLAND WATERS — LAKES AND CANALS

1. If I was a Blackbird

If I was a black-bird I'd whis-tle and sing and I'd fol-low the ship that my true love sailed in and on the top rig-ging I'd there build my nest and I'd pil-low my head on his snow-y white breast

I am a young maiden and my story is sad
For once I was courted by a brave sailor lad.
He courted me strongly by night and by day,
But now my dear sailor is gone far away.

He promised to take me to Donnybrook fair,
To buy me red ribbons to tie up my hair.
And when he'd return from the ocean so wide,
He'd take me and make me his own loving bride.

His parents they slight me and will not agree
That I and my sailor boy married should be.
But when he comes home I will greet him with joy
And I'll take to my bosom my dear sailor boy.

9

2. The Drowning of Thomas Murphy

You feel-ing heart-ed Christ-ians, I beg you now draw near, And kind-ly pay at-ten-tion to the song I'd have you hear Con-cern-ing a young he - ro of hon-oured birth and fame Who lost his life so we are told, all on the wat-ery main.

While in his native country, at home he would not stay;
In hopes to gain his fortune, this youth he put to sea.
Some time he spent in merriment; in this he took delight:
But I'll tell you how he lost his life on a lonely winter's night.

He bid farewell to Ireland: to England he took flight,
He shipped on board *The Dolphin* and she was a glorious sight
With thirty fine young heroes of courage stout and bold,
Along with Captain Wilson, who never was controlled.

'Twas from the docks of Liverpool our gallant ship set sail,
On the eighteenth day of April, with a sweet and pleasant gale –
Bound for the coast of Africa – that wild Atlantic shore:
We bid farewell to all the friends we never might see more.

When our good ship was freighted, our captain he did say:
'Cheer up my hardy British boys, make ready for the sea;
We're homeward-bound for England, the land that we adore,
And we'll drink a round of bumpers full when on our native shore.'

After an eight weeks' passage, our ship a leak she sprung;
Our captain cries: 'Cheer up, my boys, I fear we are undone.
We're far away from any port; no ship is drawing nigh;
Make ready, lower the long boats or in the deep we'll lie.'

10

'Twas then we lowered the long boats and put them off to sea;
We bid farewell to our fine ship; we could no longer stay.
We had no way to guide our boats but from the sea and sky;
No comfort could we find that day, but from the God on high.

Coming towards the evening our mate he sighted land;
He said unto his comrade-boys: 'Relief it is nigh hand.'
With courage bold we made the shore in hopes our lives to save,
But then our boat she struck the shore and was burst in by a wave.

Fourteen was our number; twelve of them were drowned:
Ten of them were washed ashore: two more could ne'er be found
There was a man amongst them, I grieve to let you know:
His name was Thomas Murphy, the pride of Curracloe.

3. Bold Denis McCarthy

Words: Trad. ballad completed by James N. Healy Music: James N. Healy

After four long days and four long nights in the chain locker he was found.
The ship was on the Atlantic waves and far from any ground.
Then up they brought McCarthy, and he hungry, stiff and sore
But ready to fight any son of a gun on *The City of Baltimore.*

The mate he came up on the deck and to the crew did say:
'Where is that Irish spalpeen who stowed himself away?'
'I'm here,' says bold McCarthy, 'and as I've said before
I'll fight any man that's fore or aft *The City of Baltimore.*'

The mate, he being a cowardly man, before him wouldn't stand;
McCarthy being a smart young man, 'twas at the mate he ran.
And with one flake of his brawny fist, this bucko he did lower,
And he stretched him senseless on the deck of *The City of Baltimore.*

The second mate and bosun came to the mate's relief;
McCarthy with his capstan bar, he soon made them retreat.
His Irish blood began to boil, and he like a lion did roar,
Saying, 'Skin and hair will fly this day on *The City of Baltimore.*'

Then to Newfoundland out they go all on the ocean green
'Now,' says McCarthy, 'there's a land I never before have seen
'Goodbye,' says he, 'my shipmates all, for I am going ashore,
To seek my fame but remember me on *The City of Baltimore.*'

And so he packed his scanty grip and down the plank did go,
They saw him plant his sturdy legs and looking to and fro;
Then he turned and waved his strong right hand, a stranger on the shore
And that's the last they heard of him on *The City of Baltimore.*

12

4. The Sailor and His Love

Words: Traditional   Air: Variant on 'The Female Smuggler'(completed by James N. Healy)

As I rov'd out one ev-'ning fair it being the sum-mertime to take the air I
spied a sail-or and a la-dy fair and I stood to lis-ten and I stood to lis-ten to
hear what they would say with a - fal - dal - day.

He said, 'Fair lady, why do you roam
For the day is spent and the night is on.'
She heaved a sigh, while tears did roll
'For my dark-eyed sailor,
For my dark-eyed sailor,
So young and stout and bold.'

''Tis seven long years since he left this land,
A ring he took from off his lily-white hand,
One half of the ring is still here with me,
But the other's rolling,
But the other's rolling
At the bottom of the sea.'

He said, 'Ye may drive him out of your mind,
Some other young man you'll surely find;
Love turns aside and cold does grow,
Like a winter's morning,
Like a winter's morning,
With the hills all white with snow.'

She said, 'I'll never forsake my dear,
Although we're parted this many a year.
Genteel he was and no rake like you,
To tempt a maiden,
To tempt a maiden,
To slight the jacket blue.'

One half of the ring did young William show,
She ran distracted in grief and woe,
Saying, 'William, William, I have gold in store
For my dark-eyed sailor,
For my dark-eyed sailor,
Has returned to me once more.'

There is a cottage by yonder lea,
This couple's married and do well agree;
So maids be loyal when your love's at sea,
For a cloudy morning,
For a cloudy morning,
Will bring a sunny day.

13

5. The Sailor Boy

Words and Music: Traditional (early 19th century)

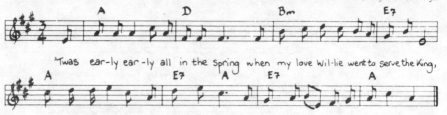

'Twas ear-ly ear-ly all in the spring when my love Wil-lie went to serve the King,

The rain was fall-ing, the wind blew high and part-ed me from my sail-or boy.

'Father, Father, come build me a boat
'Tis on the ocean I mean to float
To watch French vessels as they pass by
And to enquire for my Sailor boy.'

She was not long sailing o'er the deep
When a man-o'-warsman she chanced to meet
Saying, 'Captain, Captain, come tell me true
Is my love Willie on board with you.'

'What colour hair had your Willie dear?
What colour clothes did your Willie wear?'
'He wore a jacket of royal blue,
His hair was fair and his heart was true.'

'Indeed fair lady he is not here
That he is drowned to say I fear
'Twas on Green Island as we passed by
We lost five more and your Sailor boy.'

'Father, Father come dig me a grave
And at my head a tombstone lay
And in the centre a turtle dove
To let the world know I died of love.'

She wrung her hands and she tore her hair
Just like a lady in deep despair.
She dashed the small boat against the rocks
Saying, 'How can I live and my Willie lost.'

She wrote a letter, she wrote it long
And in the letter she wrote a song.
At every line she shed a tear
And every word she cried, 'Willie dear.'

14

6. The Saddest Breeze

The sad-dest breeze in all the land, It blew a-cross the sea; It
drove a brave ship from the strand, And bore my Hugh from me; And
long I sat be-side the rill To weep my fate a-lone, Till
leaf and flow-er from wood and hill With sum-mer beams were flown.

The gladdest breeze e'er swept the vales
Today blew from the sea;
It swelled a good ship's snowy sails,
And brought him back to me;
And now 'tis rushing wildly past.
With wintry sleet and rain,
Yet e'en I love the cold, cold blast
That brought my Hugh again!

15

7. The Sailor from Limerick Town

All you young men at-tend to me, the truth I will lay down, My par-ents reared me ten-der-ly; they lived near Lim-er-ick town For the woo-ing of a fair young maid they sent me far a-way; Ship-wrecked was I in the North Star, that now lies in the sea.

They sent me to America my fortune there to try
I shipped away in the *North Star,* that in the sea do lie
But Providence she proved kind to me, a plank brought me ashore
And I hope to see my darling girl in Limerick town once more.

When I landed on Columbia's shore no friends there could I find;
The thought of my own darling kept running through my mind.
For three long days I hardship met, as you can plainly see,
How cruel were my parents to prove my destiny.

But early the next morning just at the break o' day
A lovely maid stepped up to me and this to me did say
'My lovely youth, come tell the truth, of your sad misery,
Or are you from the heaven's above, or where is your country.'

'I am an Irishman,' I said, 'the truth I will lay down,
My parents they are wealthy and they live near Limerick town,
For the loving of a fair young maid they sent me far away,
I was shipwrecked in the *North Star,* that now lies in the sea.'

The maiden fell a-weeping, the tears fell from her eyes.
She said: 'Are you now married to that girl across the sea?
For I've got land at my command, my riches they are great;
If you join with me in wedlock bonds, you'll be lord of my estate.'

16

'To join with you in wedlock bonds is a thing I ne'er shall do
For I have fairly promised, by an oath that I'll keep true
That I'll wed with my fair one is the oath that will remain
There's not another on this earth shall e'er my favour gain.'

This maiden fell in deep despair and this unto me did say,
'Here is one hundred pounds in gold, to bring you o'er the sea
Since love, I see, is worth far more than any earthly store
May the heaven protect you o'er the sea to your Irish girl once more.'

8. Charming Mary Neal

I'm —— a bold un-daunt-ed youth, my name is John Mac Cann. I'm
a nat-ive of Don - e - gal, con-ven - ient to Stra-bane; For
the steal-ing of an heir - ess, I lie in Lif-ford Jail. Her
fa - ther swears he'll hang me for his daught-er Ma-ry Neal.

Whilst I lay in irons cold, my love she came to me:
'Don't fear my father's anger, for I will set you free.'
Her father gave consent to let me out on bail,
And I was to stand trial for his daughter Mary Neal.

Her father kept her close confined, for fear I should her see,
And on my trial day, was my prosecutor to be;
But like a loyal lover, to appear she did not fail,
She freed me from all dangers; she's my charming Mary Neal.

With wrath and indignation, her father loud did call,
And when my trial was over, I approached the garden wall,
My well-known voice soon reached her ears, which echoed hill and dale,
Saying, 'You're welcome here, my Johnny dear,' says charming Mary Neal.

We both sat on a sunny bank, and there we talked awhile.
He says, 'My dear, if you will comply, I'll free you from exile.
The *Shamrock* is ready from Derry to set sail;
So come with me, off to Quebec, my charming Mary Neal.'

She gave consent, and back she went, and stole the best of clothes,
And to no one in the house her secret she made known;
Five hundred pounds of ready gold from her father she did steal,
And that was twice I did elope with charming Mary Neal.

Our coach it was got ready to Derry for to go,
And there we bribed the coachman for to let no one know;
He said he would keep secret, and never would reveal.
So off to Derry there I went with charming Mary Neal.

It was to Captain Nelson our passage money paid,
And in the town of Derry it was under cover laid.
We joined our hands in wedlock bands before we did set sail.
And her father's wrath I value not. I love my Mary Neal.

It was over the proud and swelling seas our ship did gently glide,
And on our passage to Quebec, six weeks a matchless tide;
Until we came to Whitehead Beach we had no cause to wail,
On Crossford Bay I thought that day I lost my Mary Neal.

On the ninth of June, in the afternoon, a heavy fog came on;
The captain cries, 'Look out, my boys! I fear we are all gone.'
Our vessel on a sandy bank was driven by a gale,
And forty more washed overboard, along with Mary Neal.

With the help of boats and the ship's crew, five hundred they were saved
And forty more of them also have met a watery grave.
I soon spied her yellow locks come floating down the waves:
I jumped into the boiling deep and saved my Mary Neal.

Her father wrote a letter as you may understand,
That if I would go back again he would give me all his land.
I wrote him back an answer, and that without fail,
'That I'm the heir of your whole estate, by your daughter Mary Neal.'

18

9. Your Faithful Sailor Boy

'Twas in a gale, that the ship set sail; the lass was standing by,
She watched the vessel out of sight, and the tears stood in her eyes.
She prayed to Him in Heaven above to guide him on his way,
And a parting word from her own true love did echo o'er the bay.

Chorus:

19

The ship returned, but sad to say, without her sailor boy,
He died at sea while under weigh, and the flags were half-mast high
And when his comrades came ashore; they told her that he was dead,
And in a letter he had wrote the last lines sadly read:

Chorus: Farewell, farewell, my own true love, on earth we'll meet no more
I hope we'll meet in Heaven above on that bright and happy shore:
I hope we'll meet in that bright land, that land beyond the sky
Where you will never be parted from your faithful sailor boy.

10. Across the Western Ocean

The land of Promise there you'll see
Amelia, whar' you bound to?
I'm bound across that western sea,
To join the Irish Army.

To Liverpool I'll take my way
Amelia, whar' you bound to?
To Liverpool, that Yankee school
Across the Western Ocean.

There's Liverpool Pat with his tarpaulin hat
Amelia, whar' you bound to?
And Yankee John the packet rat,
Across the Western Ocean

Beware those packet ships I pray
Amelia, whar' you bound to?
They steal your stores and clothes away
Across the Western Ocean.

11. Paddy Doyle

To my way..a..y..ay..ah
(1) We'll all drink brandy and gin.
(2) We'll all throw dirt (?) at the cook
(3) We'll all shave under the chin.

12. Commodore Jack Barry

Words: William Collins   Music: James N. Healy

One eve as day was dy - ing and sink-ing in - to night, With the
Brit-ish en - sign fly - ing the Sib-yl came in sight. The
Eng - lish cap - tain hailed us as he down up-on us bore, And
proud-ly an - swered Bar - ry our brave old Com-mo-dore.

'This is the ship, *Alliance*, from Philadelphia town;
She proudly bids defiance to England's King and crown.
As captain of the deck I stand to guard her banner true;
Half-Yankee and half-Irishman, what tyrant's slave are you?'

Then with the voice of thunder our guns began the fight,
Though battling against number and the foeman's fleet in sight;
For the *Hudson* and the *Shannon* 'gainst the minions of the crown,
We fought them till our cannon brought the British ensign down.

Says the Commodore: 'We'll take her from before their very eyes;
With another broadside rake her and we'll carry off the prize.'
Then our round shot went careering through their rigging and their spars,
And our crew began a cheering for the Yankee stripes and stars.

And streaming on the breeze aloft it waved in all its pride
Above the foeman's captured craft now sailing by our side.
Oh how our gallant seamen cheered just as the sun went down,
And our good vessel homeward steered for Philadelphia town.

13. Captain Coulston

The number of his passengers was three hundred and sixty-two;
And they were all teetotallers, excepting one or two,
The lemonade was passed around, to nourish them at sea,
And Father Mathew's medals they wore unto Amerikay.

The weather was as charming as ever you saw before;
For twenty days of pleasure we never thought of shore.
The captain and his lady fair, were seen on deck each day
To crown our hearts with merriment while sailing on the sea.

It was on the twelfth of April, just at the fall of night
Our captain went around his ship to see if all was right.
He said, 'Brave boys, do not go down, you need not think of sleep
For in a few short moments we'll be slumbering in the deep.

'A pirate ship is coming up from o'er the western sea,
To rob us of our property as we go to Amerikay.'
The pirate ship she then came up, and ordered us to stand:
'Your gold and precious loading, this moment I demand.

'Your gold and precious loading, resign to us this day,
For if not, one soul you'll never bring unto Amerikay.'
Then out spoke Captain Coulston, unto his jovial crew
Saying, 'We will fight until we die; we've nothing else to do.'

22

Then out spoke Captain Coulston, that hero stout and bold:
''Tis in the deep we all will sleep, before we'll be controlled.'
This bloody battle then commenced, the blood in streams did flow,
Undaunted were our Irish boys, who did them overthrow.

There was a young man on the deck with his true love by his side
With courage bold they fought their way along the bulwark side.
She cried, 'My gallant hero, I'll shortly end this strife.'
And with a pocket pistol ball, she took the pirate captain's life.

Then cried the women and the children as in the hold they lay
While the captain and his Irish boys showed the pirates gallant play.
'Well done, well done,' brave Coulston cried. 'Well done my lady too.
Your aim has proved so deadly, you've shot the pirate captain through.'

Now to conclude and finish, the truth I will tell you
Our losses were not many, they being only one or two.
The pirate ship surrendered just at the break of day
And we brought her as a prisoner unto Amerikay.

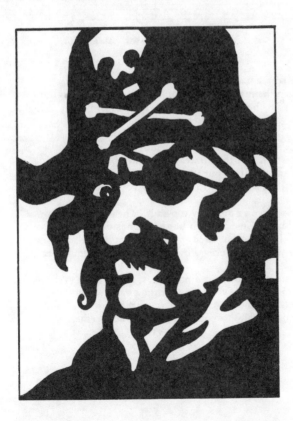

14. Kelly the Pirate

We scarce had been sailing for days two or three,
When the man from our top-mast strange colours did see.
He came bearing down on us with his main-sheet so high,
And out from his mizen-peak those colours did fly.

Our mate he came aft and he judged her all round:
'This is Kelly, the Pirate, I'll bet fifty pound.'
He said: 'Drop your top-sails and heave your ship to,
For I am a packet with letters for you.'

'Now I won't drop my top-sails or heave my ship to;
It'll be in some harbour but not 'longside you.'
He chased and he fired, but he did not prevail,
For the bold *Princess Royal* soon showed them her tail.

Come down to your dinner boys, come down every man;
Come down to your grog for the pirate is gone.
Half barrels of rum like salt water did flow:
Drink a health to your wives and your sheethearts also.

15. Fineen O'Driscoll, The Rover

Words: R. W. Joyce   Air: 'The Groves of Blackpool'

The Saxons of Cork and Moyallo*
They harried his lands with their powers;
He gave them a taste of his cannon,
And drove them like wolves from
                              [his towers;
The men of Clan London brought out
Their strong fleet to make him a slave;
They met him by Mizen's wild headland,
And the sharks gnawed their bones 'neath
Chorus: [the wave.

Long time in that old battered castle,
Or out on the waves with his clan.
He feasted and ventured and conquered,
But ne'er struck his colours to man
In a fight 'gainst the foes of his country.
He died as a brave man should die,
And he sleeps 'neath the waters of Cleena,
Where the waves sing his caoine† to the sky.
Chorus:

* Moyallo: Mallow
† caoine: pronounced 'keen'.

25

16. The Sack of Baltimore

Words: *Thomas Davis*   Air: *'Cois Laoi na Sreabh'*

The Sum-mer sun is fall-ing soft On Car-bry's hun-dred isles The Sum-mer sun is gleam-ing still Thro' Gab-riel's rough de-files old In-ish-er-kins crumb-led fane Looks like a moult-ing bird; And in a calm and sleep-y swell The oc-ean tide is heard. The hook-ers lie up-on the beach; The child-ren cease their play; The gos-sips leave their lit-tle inn, The house-holds kneel to pray — And full of love and peace and rest Its dail-y la-bour o'er Up-on that cos-y creek there lay The town of Bal-ti-more.

A deeper rest, a starry trance,
Has come with midnight there;
No sound, except that throbbing wave,
In earth, or sea, or air.
The massive capes and ruined towers,
Seem conscious of the calm;
The fibrous sod and stunted trees
Are breathing heavy balm.

So still the night, these two long barques
Round Dunashad that glide,
Must trust their ears – methinks not few –
Against the ebbing tide;
Oh! some sweet mission of true love
Must urge them to the shore –
They bring some lover to his bride
Who sighs in Baltimore.

All, all asleep within each roof
Along that rocky street,
And these must be the lover's friends
With gentle gliding feet –
A stifled gasp! a dreamy noise
'The roof is in a flame!'
From out their beds, and to their doors,
Rush maid and sire and dame.

And meet, upon the threshold stone,
The gleaming sabre fall,
And o'er each black and bearded face,
The white or crimson shawl –
The yell of 'Allah!' breaks above,
The pray'r and shriek, and roar –
O blessed God! the Algerine
Is lord of Baltimore!

17. Gráinnu Mhaol
(Grace O'Malley)

Words: P. J. McCall Air: trad. ('Mo Theaglach')

'By stout Car - rig - a - hul - la my war ves - sels ride, Like Swans they are breast - ing the swift ebb - ing tide: There is wrath for the Sax - on and ruth for the Gael In yon proud Span - ish gal - leys!' said Gráinn - u Waile. Sing Bo - bar o! Do - dar - o! Gráinn - u Waile - Sing, gal - leys and Gaels all read - y to sail, To sweep the salt seas from Cape Clear to Kin - sale; For the Queen of the oc - ean is Gráinn - u Waile!

'Then Queen Bess, the dear virgin, wrote friendly and fond
For sweet Grace, her kind coz, to go journey beyond;
So I doffed my steel barradh and donned my silk veil,
And I went a cuckooien!' said Gráinnu Waile.

'Mo Fuil! could you note how she wondered at me,
With my loose yellow mantle and blue bodice free;
She had pilfered, herself, every bone from a whale,
To bind up her long body!' said Gráinnu Waile.

'Bess offered me honours – to me, her peer!
Then she offered protection – whom, whom do I fear?
So she offered me peace – sure we're used to a gale
In stout Carrig-a-hulla!' said Gráinnu Waile.

'Then she gave me a spaniel – I smothered a curse;
For I had my own babe for my bosom to nurse –
No shivering pet that slinks down to his tail,
But a wolf-hound of Connacht!' said Gráinnu Waile.

'Bess parleyed for peace, yet base Bingham is out,
With full many a Sassenach churleen and lout;
But, dar Dia! if Clann Leeam he dares to assail,
There'll be blood on my bonnet!' said Gráinnu Waile.

18. The Boys of Ballinamore

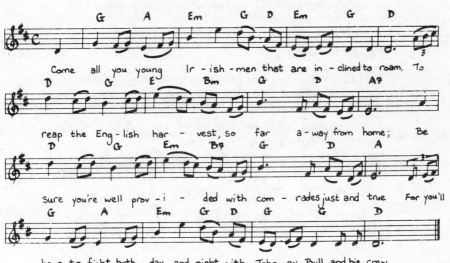

When we left home for Dublin, the weather it was fair.
And when we got on board the ship we gave a hearty cheer!
Hurrah! my boys! for Paddy's land, the place we all adore,
The heavens smile on every child that loves the Shamrock shore.

We sailed away from Dublin quay and ne'er received a shock
'Till we landed safe on shore once more one side of Clarence Dock,
Where numbers of our Irish boys they met us in the town,
And 'Hurrah for Paddy's lovely land' was the toast that went around.

With one consent away we went to drink strong ale and wine,
And each man drank a favourite health to the girl he left behind.
We drank and sung till the ale-house rung, despising Érin's foes,
Or any man that hates the land where Patrick's Shamrock grows.

Next morning by the break of day, as quickly you shall hear,
One hundred strong we marched along without either dread or fear,
Each man had his blackthorn stick he brought from Paddy's land,
And a hook that gleamed like polished steel or silver in his hand.

For three days we tramp'd away high wages for to find,
And on the following evening we came to a railway line;
The navvies they came up to us and loudly they did rail,
They curs'd and damn'd the Paddies and the sons of Granuail.

Up starts Barney Walsh and says, 'Boys what do you mean?
Are we not men as well as you and hate a coward's name.
So Faugh-a-Ballagh! clear the way! or some of you must fall,
For here we stand true Irishmen that never fear'd a call.'

These English navvies curs'd and swore they'd kill us ten times o'er,
They would make us remember Banamuck and Glevnamore,
Brave Father Maguire, just and true, they curs'd his blessed remains,
Which made our County Leitrim boys to burn for revenge.

Up steps Barney Riley and he knocks their ganger down.
The bricks and stones they flew like hail in showers they came down.
We fought from half-past four until the sun was going to set,
When Riley says, 'My Irish boys, I fear we will be beat.'

'Come now with me, my countrymen resume the fight once more.
We'll assail the foes on every side more desperate than before,
We'll let them know before we go, we'd rather fight than fly,
For at the worst of times, my boys, you know we'd rather die.'

We sallied back with Barney and challenged another round.
Like Samson with the Philistines we laid them on the ground.
We fought our way, the lifelong day to force them to give o'er.
We proved to them we were Irishmen from sweet old Ballinamore.

When the fight commenced the second time 'tis there you'd see some fun,
The hooks and sticks were flashing, till the navvies were undone,
The cowardly clan away they ran, their heads and arms sore,
They'll remember Barney Riley and the boys of Ballinamore.

So here's long life to Riley, M'Cormick and M'Cabe
And likewise brave M'Gorner who never was afraid;
And every man from Paddy's land that fought upon that day,
And forced those English navvies in gangs to run away.

19. The Widow of Donaghadee

Words: Traditional Air: 'Toor-al-i-ay'

There was an old wid-ow in Don-agh-a-dee, And in her back gar-den a row of plum trees, But the wid-ow's big dog was a-tied to its roots And the town la-dies they wore a nip of its tooths. Too-ra-loo,————— Too-ra-lee,————— Oh, it's six miles from Ban-gor to Don-agh-a-dee.

So she bought a wee horse and she went thro' the town
Selling apples and oranges all the way round.
And she'd crack her old whip and sit twisting her thumbs
Till the town folk were shy of her garden and plums.
Chorus:

But one day a ship sailed in close to the quay,
It had run from a voyage far away on the sea,
The poor half-starved sailors they made for the shore,
And dropped like the devil on the old widow's door.
Chorus:

She gave them some soup and she gave them some tea,
She dry baked the oaten as quick as could be,
A quart of fine whiskey as they picked up the crumbs,
Then from her back garden she brought in her plums.
Chorus:

31

They ate all those plums till their tummies were sore,
In anger the skipper made for the back door.
He cursed and he raved and he tore up the root
And a hundred bright sov'rigns he picked up as loot.
Chorus:

And now all you listeners take warning from me,
I sailed round the world and on many a sea.
Many plums I have sampled as ripe as could be,
But the best plums of all came from Donaghadee.
Chorus:

20. The Loss of the Hantoon

At-tend ye sons of Nep-tune that roam the an-gry seas And
all ye jol-ly sail-or lads that are moored from dan-ger free I
ask your kind at-ten-tion to my sad and dole-ful tune Of the
mel-an-cho-ly ac-ci-dent of the Wex-ford barque Han-toon.

On the twenty-sixth of December, I mean to let you hear
Calm were the waves and beautiful, the sky was bright and clear
In pride and stately grandeur our gallant barque did glide,
With reflections of her beauty on the silvery flowing tide.

The elevating joys of home did o'er our senses steal
John Cullen with his steady hand did safely steer the wheel.
Delightfully he viewed her track, crowned by the billows foam
As by the gentle breezes our ship was wafted home.

On the ensuing morning before the dawn appeared,
Five and a half knots sailing, east-north-east we steered.
The wind was in our favour, our happiness to crown
When this cruel British monster on us came bearing down.

The signal for 'All hands on deck' immediately did sound
And from his peaceful slumber brave Captain Neill did bound.
He tried his whole endeavour to save his ship and crew
But those cursed, heartless tyrants had cut our barque in two.

Then her mast came crashing down, likewise each spar and sail
And from the opening gulf beneath there rose a dismal wail.
To search for men was fruitless in the boats that put to sea.
The mountain waves rolled over them and sealed their destiny.

Eleven were our good ship's crew, but only seven were found;
The other three with Captain Neill were killed as well as drowned.
Near the rock-bound coast of Portugal each lifeless body rolls
May He, whose Voice the waves obey, have mercy on their souls.

The thought of coming home again was painful to our mind,
In leaving loving comrades and ship-mates far behind.
Far away from home and country with their gallant barque they sleep
In the broad Atlantic's bosom full fifty fathoms deep.

Now to conclude and finish, too far my lines have run;
To the owner and the gallant crew may justice soon be done;
And may the perpetrator's lot be on the gallows tree,
Who thought to send a whole ship's crew into Eternity.

21a. Báidín Fheidhlimidh

Traditional: N.W. Coast

Báidín Fheidhlimidh d'ímigh go Toraigh
Báidín Fheidhlimidh 's Feidhlimidh ann.

Báidín Fheidhlimidh briseadh i dToraigh í
Báidín Fheidhlimidh 's Feidhlimidh ann.

Codetta: Báidín Fheidhlimidh ...
Báidín Fheidhlimidh ...

21b. Phelim's Wee Boat

English translation by James N. Healy

Phelim's boat will go sailing to Gowla.
'Tis Phelim's wee boat, and with Phelim we'll sail.

Phelim's boat will go sailing to Tory.
'Tis Phelim's wee boat, and with Phelim we'll sail.

Chorus:
Boat of neatness; boat of sweetness
Neat and sweet the boat of Phelim is,
Tidy, and fine, with a beautiful line.
'Tis Phelim's wee boat, and with Phelim we'll sail.

Phelim's wee boat was wrecked out on Tory
Phelim was steering and no one else there.

Codetta: Boat of Phelim ...
          Boat of Phelim ...

22. The Rescue of the Vivandiere

Traditional

Come all ye gal-lant sea-men bold of high and low de-gree And
like-wise pay at-ten-tion and lis-ten un-to me; 'Tis
of the sea that you will hear and you'll give a ring-ing cheer All
for the no-ble res-cue of the gal-lant Viv-an-diere.

This was a new built vessel, material good and sound;
A circumnavigator, to sail the ocean round.
She was manned by noble seamen as I do now suspect,
But they left her on Blackwater Bank, a dire and total wreck.

The tide going round the Raven Point, the owners they may thank;
For 'twas on the flood of water she wafted from the Bank.
Forlorn and abandoned, the truth I now will say:
She drifted north before the wind all out from Wexford quay.

The men from Tinnaberna bold, to danger could not yield.
For fearless were their forebearers on either flood or field.
They launched their boats without delay, no danger did they fear;
And one of these bold seamen stepped aboard the *Vivandiere*.

Myles Brien, he mounted on a horse, to Wexford he did steer,
Saying: 'Eleven men and my brother Jem, are aboard the *Vivandiere*',
Tom King, he took the helm just at the gloom of night,
Saying: 'Cheer up, my boys, for Wextord,' and they raised the Tuskar Light.

When the news of this disaster had reached old Wexford town,
The tug-boat and her gallant crew, with courage hastened down,
To help those worthy fishermen, she came without delay,
And brought the gallant *Vivandiere* safe into Wexford Quay.

36

23. The Sorrowful Fate of O'Brien

You landsmen all on you I call and gallant seamen too Till
I relate the hardships great that lately we went through;
From Limerick in the breeze to St. John's we set sail, On the
twenty seventh of November in a sweet and pleasant gale.

It happened many miles from land, on her beam end she lay,
Our fore and main mast instantly we had to cut away;
When her masts went overboard, to rights she came again,
Three foot of water in her hold till daylight did remain.

Early the next morning we viewed our awful state:
Ben Cusack he was drowned and Griffin, our first mate.
Down below we could not go where our fresh water lay,
And as for meat we'd none to eat, for all was washed away.

All we got safe from out the wreck was three bottles of Port Wine,
And every time that we got weak, we took a drop each time.
We had not water for to drink but what fell from the sky,
And no dry spot then could be got to either sit or lie.

On the third day of December, it being on the ninth day,
Without tasting any kind of food; the hunger upon us did prey
Our captain cried: 'Cheer up my boys; let those four boys cast lots
They have no wives: to save our lives one of these four must die.'

While lots they were preparing, these poor unfortunate boys
Stood gazing at each other with salt tears in their eyes
A bandage o'er O'Brien's eyes they quickly then did tie
For the second lot that was pulled up said O'Brien was to die.

He said unto his comrade boys: 'Now let my mother know
The cruel death I did sustain, when you to Limerick go.'
Then John O'Gorman he was called to bleed him in the vein
Twice he tried to take his blood, but it was all in vain.

Our captain cries: 'Cheer up, my boys, this work will never do;
O'Gorman you must cut his throat, or else you will die too.'
The trembling cook, he took the knife, which sore did him confound.
He cut his throat and drank his blood as it flowed from the wound.

24. The Sinking of the Muirchu

Words: James N. Healy Air: 'The Boys of Wexford'

She was a rare and fair boat She was a fair and rare boat She
was a blid-dy quare boat The good old Muir - - chu. I
board - ed her in Haul - bow-line With me life-belt in me hand All
for the cause of free - dom And me dear ould na - tive land. We
joined the Muir - chu me boys To fight thro' shot and shell — We
got half-shot in Cobh, me boys To brave the o - cean's swell.

We started out for Dublin Town
The Captain steered us straight
But when we reached the ocean
The poor oul' ship was bate
She took one look at the rolling sea
And knew she could not do
So off the coast of Wexford
We lost the *Muirchu*.
We lost the *Muirchu*, me boys
Tho' she sailed with might and main
From Haul-bowline to Dublin Town
For scrap at Hammond Lane.

The *Muirchu* got lost at sea
Tho' we searched everywhere
And when we turned and swam for shore
We could not find her there.
But she'll live in song and story
The greatest ship of all
The guardian of our harbours
The Flagship of the Dáil.
The good old *Muirchu*, me boys
Will never be a slave
For off the coast of Wexford
She found a sailor's grave.

25. The Irish Rover

Words: Traditional   Music: 19th century

Donoghue and MacHugh came from Red Waterloo,
And O'Neill and MacFlail from the Rhine,
There was Ludd and MacGludd from the land of the flood
Pat Malone, Mike MacGowan and O'Brien,
Bould MacGee, MacEntee and big Neill from Tigree
And Michael O'Dowd from Dover
And a man from Turkestan sure his name was Kid MacCann
Was the skipper of the *Irish Rover*.

We had one million bags of the best Sligo rags,
We had two million barrels of bones,
We had three million sides from old blind horse hides,
We had four million bags full of stones,
We had five million dogs and six million hogs,
And seven million bundles of clover.
We had eight million bales of old billy goat tails,
In the hold of the *Irish Rover*.

Oh! we sailed seven years and the measles broke out,
And the ship lost her way in a fog,
And the whole of the crew was reduced unto two
Just meself and the skipper's old dog.
And we struck on a rock with a terrible shock
And, Lord, she rolled right over.
Turned nine times right around; the old dog he got drowned
I'm the last of the *Irish Rover*.

*Final
Chorus:*

Fare thee well, my own true one, I'm going far from you
And I will swear by the stars above, forever I'll be true;
But as I part it will break my heart, and when the trip is over,
I'll roam again in true Irish style aboard the *Irish Rover*.

26. St Patrick's Arrival

(or **The Invention of Punch**)

Words: 'Lanner de Waltram' (Captain Wood)
Air: 'Patrick's day in the Morning'

'Your wig, white as flax,
Makes me bold for to ax
It's who are you, what are you, from whence that you came?'
Then the Other replied,
'I came in the last tide;
I'm a saint come to serve you, and Patrick's my name.
With the crook in my hand
I'll roam over this land,
And I'll draw yee together like mountainy sheep;

41

I'll card off the sins
That stick close in your skins:
'Tis ther'll be a revel
While I bate the Devil
A beast with long horns, and black as a sweep.
Go, lie down in clover,
Till the skrimmage is over.
For its Patrick's day in the morning.'

With a thundering polthogue,
And the toe of his brogue,
The Saint kicked the Divil beyond the Black sea.
Then he spoke to the nation –
'My sweet congregation,
You've spirits remaining that's stronger than he;
Sure ye knows what I means –
They bewilder your brains –
They're as clear as the streamlet that flows through the green.
But stronger than Samson,
Who pulled post and lamps on
His enemies' head,
'Till he kilt them stone-dead;
And the name of the spirit I mean is poteen,
I exhort ye, don't stick, sirs,
To those Devil's elixirs,
Of a Patrick's day in the morning!'

The Saint fell asleep
And the Spalpeens all creep
For some cruiskeens of whiskey nate and unmastered
With this essence of sins
Soon they filled up their skins:
When the Saint he awoke, they were plastered.
As fuddled they lay,
Says the Saint, 'There's a way
To wean them: I'll mawkish stuff put in each bottle;
And when they awake,
If a swig they should take,
Oh, dear! 'twill disgust them.
I think I may trust them,
They'll vow that no more shall pass down through their throttle
Sweet sugar I'll pour;
Squeeze a lemon so sour,
On Patrick's day in the morning!'

He went off – they awoke,
Each cruiskeen did smoke
Like the flue of a steamer – each pounced on his drink.
Their shewing grimaces,
Their making their faces,
Was ext – or – dinary but, what do you think?
With features awry,
In a hogshead hard by,
Each emptied his bottle, though dying with thirst;
Till one, dry as sponge,
At the tub made a plunge,
Where the sour, and the sweet,
And the whiskey did meet;
And he swigged off this physic, till ready to burst,
By the side of this mixture
Each man grew a fixture,
On St Patrick's day in the morning!

When St Patrick came back,
'Och!' says he, 'ye vile pack
Of the spawn of the Druids – ye villanous bunch!'
But a noise, as from Babel,
Here made him unable
To hear his own voice, though he said, 'Is the Punch' –
Eon, he'd have added,
But the Spalpeens were madded,
Their howls cut short questions, remark or reply.
'Ay, Punch,' they roared out,
With an earth-shaking shout,
'Is the name of this thing
That is drink for a king,
Or the mouth of a Druid, if ever he's dry;
It would coax pipe-shank'd Death
For to let one take breath
On St Patrick's day in the morning!'

27. Sailing in the Lowlands Low

Words: P. J. McCall Air: Traditional

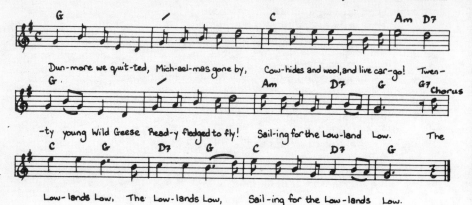

Dun-more we quit-ted, Mich-ael-mas gone by, Cow-hides and wool, and live car-go! Twen--ty young Wild Geese Read-y fledged to fly! Sail-ing for the Low-land Low. The Low-lands Low, The Low-lands Low, Sail-ing for the Low-lands Low.

Shaun Paor's the skipper,
From the church of Crook –
Piery keeps log for his father!
Crew all from Bannow,
Fethard and the Hook –
Sailing in the Lowlands Low!

These twenty Wild Geese
Gave Queen Anne the slip,
Crossing to Lewey in Flanders:
He and Jack Malbrook
Both are in a grip,
Fighting in the Lowlands Low!

Close lay a rover
Off the Isle of Wight,
Either a Salee or Saxon!
Out through a sea mist
We bade them good night,
Sailing for the Lowlands Low!

Ready with priming
We'd our galliot gun:
Muskets and pikes in good order!
We should be riddled –
Captives would be none!
Death! or else the Lowlands Low!

Pray, holy Brendan,
Turk or Algerine,
Dutchman nor Saxon may sink us!
We'll bring Geneva
Rack and Rhenish wine
Safely from the Lowlands Low!

28. The Lowlands of Holland

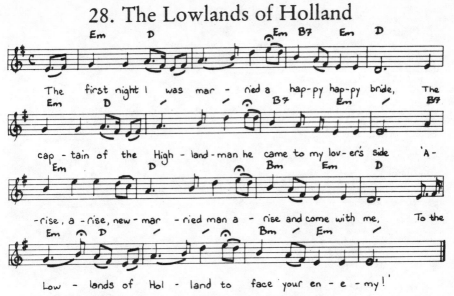

The first night I was mar - ried a hap-py hap-py bride, The
cap - tain of the High - land-man he came to my lov-er's side 'A -
-rise, a - rise, new - mar - ried man a - rise and come with me, To the
Low - lands of Hol - land to face your en - e - my!

I held my love in my arms still thinking he might stay,
But the captain gave another shout; he was forced to go away:
"Tis many a blithe young married man this night must go with me
To the Lowlands of Holland to fight the enemy!'

Oh! Holland is a wond'rous place, and in it grows much green
It's a wild habitation for my true love to lie in.
The wild flowers grow most plentuous there, and fruit on every tree
But the Lowlands of Holland are between my love and me!

They took my love to a gallant ship, a ship of noble fame,
With four-and-twenty seamen bold to steer across the main:
The storm then began to rise, and the seas began to shout.
'Twas then my love and his gallant ship were sorely tossed about.

Says the mother to the daughter, 'What makes you so lament?
Is there ne'er a man in Ireland who will please your discontent.'
'There are men enough in Ireland, but none at all for me
I only love but one man, and he's across the sea.

'I'll wear not shoe or stocking, or comb put in my hair,
Nor fire bright nor candle light shall show my beauty rare.
Nor will I wed with any man until the day I die
Since the Lowlands of Holland are between my love and I.'

29. Van Dieman's Land

Moderato

Come all you gal-lant poach-ers that ram-ble void of care — That walk out on a moon-light night with your dog and gun and snare; The hare and loft-y pheas-ant you have at your com-mand Not think-ing of your last car-eer up-on Van Die-man's Land.

Poor Thomas Brown from Nenagh town, Jack Murphy and poor Joe
Were three determined poachers as the country well does know.
By the keepers of the land, my boys, one night we were trepanned
And for fourteen years transported unto Van Dieman's Land.

The first day that we landed upon that fatal shore
The planters came around us, and we might be twenty score.
They ranked us off like horses and they sold us out of hand
And they yoked us to the plough, brave boys, to plough Van Dieman's Land.

The cottages we live in here are built with sods of clay.
We have rotten straw for bedding, but we dare not say them nay.
Our cots we fence with firing and slumber when we can
To keep the wolves and dogs from us in Van Dieman's Land.

Oft times when I do slumber I have a pleasant dream
With my sweet girl sitting close to me near a purling stream;
I am roaming through old Ireland with my true love by the hand –
But waken broken-hearted upon Van Dieman's Land.

God bless our wives and families, likewise that happy shore,
That isle of sweet contentment which we shall see no more.
As for wretched females see them we seldom can
There are twenty men for one woman in Van Dieman's Land.

There was a girl from Nenagh town, Peg Brophy was her name,
For fourteen years transported was, we all well knew the same;
But the planter bought her freedom and married her out of hand,
And she gives us good usage upon Van Dieman's Land.

But fourteen years is a long time, and that is our fatal doom –
For nothing else but poaching, for that is all we done:
You would leave off both dog and gun and poaching every man
If you but knew the hardship that's in Van Dieman's Land.

Oh, if I had a thousand pounds all laid out in my hand
I'd give it all for liberty if that I could command,
Again to Ireland I'd return and be a happy man
And bid adieu to poaching and to Van Dieman's Land.

30. Lonely Banna Strand

'Twas on Good Fri-day morn-ing all in the month of May a
Ger-man ship was sig-nall'd be-yond there in the bay. We've
twen-ty thous-and rif-les here all read-y for to land But no
ans-w'ring sig-nal came from the lone-ly Ban-na Strand.

A motor-car was dashing through the early morning gloom,
A sudden crash, and in the sea they went to meet their doom,
Two Irish lads lay dying there just like their hopes so grand.
They could not give the signal now from lonely Banna Strand.

'No signal answers from the shore,' Sir Roger sadly said,
'No comrades here to welcome me, alas! they must be dead;
But I must do my duty and at once I mean to land,'
So in a boat he pulled ashore to lonely Banna Strand.

The German ships were lying there with rifles in galore.
Up came a British ship and spoke, 'No Germans reach the shore;
You are our Empire's enemy, and so we bid you stand.
No German foot shall e'er pollute the lonely Banna Strand.

They sailed for Queenstown Harbour. Said the Germans: 'We're undone,
The British are our masters man for man and gun for gun.
We've twenty thousand rifles here, but they never will reach land.
We'll sink them all and bid farewell to lonely Banna Strand.'

The R.I.C. were hunting for Sir Roger high and low,
They found him at McKenna's Fort, said they: 'You are our foe.'
Said he, 'I'm Roger Casement, I came to my native land,
I meant to free my countrymen on the lonely Banna Strand.'

They took Sir Roger prisoner and sailed for London Tower,
And in the Tower they laid him as a traitor to the Crown.
Said he, 'I am no traitor,' but his trial he had to stand.
For bringing German rifles to the lonely Banna Strand.

'Twas in an English prison that they led him to his death.
'I'm dying for my country,' he said with his last breath.
He's buried in a prison yard far from his native land
The wild waves sing his Requiem on lonely Banna Strand.

31. The Kinsale Ballad

Words and Music: James N. Healy

Long a-go in sweet kin-sale Ire-land lost her lib-er-ty When King
James had set his sail Past the Sov-ereigns to the sea. So the
Wild Geese flew a-way; Of their flight we sad-ly sing, Sars-field's
ships were on the say And the Geese were on the wing.

It was many years before
That the Spaniards quartered there
But the English beat O'Neill
And our Irish hopes lay bare.
It was vain for us to sing
Of O'Donnell's bravery
When the Geese were on the wing
And the ships were on the sea.

For in Spain O'Donnell died
And in France King James was laid
And the shade of Erin grieved
That her cause had been betrayed
But the years of grief and tears
Brought the hope of O'Connell and Tone
And through Collins and thro' Pearse
Ireland now has gained her own.

Where the Bandon meets the sea
Lies Kinsale so pleasant there
Quiet town and winding streets,
And the harbour waters fair:
For her country now is free,
There is no more need to roam,
Little ships are on the sea
And the Geese can now come home.

32. The County of Mayo

Words: George Fox   Air: Red Regan and the Nun

On the deck of Pat-rick Lynch-'s boat I sit in wo'-ful plight Thro' my
sigh-ing all the wea-ry day And weep-ing all the night; were it
not that full of sor-row from My peo-ple forth I go —— By the
bless-ed sun 'tis roy-al-ly I'd sing thy praise May-o.

When I dwelt at home in plenty,
And my gold did much abound,
In the company of fair young maids
The Spanish ale went round.
'Tis a bitter change from those gay days
That now I'm forced to go,
And must leave my bones in Santa Cruz
Far from my own Mayo.

They are altered girls in Irrul now;
'Tis proud they've grown and high,
With their hair-bags and their top-knots,
For I pass their buckles by;
But it's little now I heed their airs
For God will have it so,
That I must depart for foreign lands,
And leave my sweet Mayo.

'Tis my grief that Patrick Loughlin
Is not Earl in Irrul still,
And that Brian Duff no longer rules
As lord upon the hill;
And that Colonel Hugh O'Grady
Should be lying dead and low,
And I sailing, sailing swiftly
From the County of Mayo.

33. My Love Nell

Words: Unknown Air: Traditional 'The Tailor and the Piper'

Mind, you boys, both far and near
   And a warning take by me.
One bird in the hand you will understand
   Is worth thirty thousand million on the tree.
Persuade you may to name the day,
   Say, 'Your time ma'am suits me,'
Or as slippery as an eel they will turn on their heel,
   And be off to Amerikay.   *Refrain:*

When we got to the church I was left in the lurch,
   But let that one go by,
When we got to the door, Nell said she was poor
   'Oh,' says I, 'then, Nell, goodbye.'
'You're an Irish girl, faith, I know well,
   But ye won't come over me.'
   'Then,' says Nell, 'D'ye mind, faith, I leave ye behind,
   And I'll sail for Amerikay.'   *Refrain:*

34. The Glasgow

Words: possibly John Williams of Cootehill

All you who love your nat-ive land and mean to em-i-grate while draw near and you shall hear what hap-pened here of late To tell the hard-ships I went through some pag-es it would fill When I was forced to leave my home, that place called sweet Coote-hill.

John Williams is my name, this truth I'll ne'er deny;
My friends they banished me away, I'll tell the reason why –
Because I would not break the vows I made unto my dear,
They tore me from the arms of my charming Sally Greer.

Straight away to Liverpool my friends did me convey,
And in the *Glasgow* to New York my passage they did pay
Along with Captain Robinson and sixteen of a crew
We set out for America our fortune to pursue.

'Twas on the eighth of February our gallant ship set sail
Bound for the city of New York, with a sweet and pleasant gale.
On the midnight of the seventh day, before our captain went to rest
He called unto his chief-mate and made him this behest:

'Take you charge of the vessel, and of yon rocks keep clear.
And beat about the Irish coast till daylight doth appear.'
Our chief-mate took the orders, but he did not them obey
And by neglect he let the ship go quite out of her way.

Early the following morning, about half-past four o'clock,
Our gallant ship with all her might came on a sunken rock.
These rocks are called 'The Barrels'; they're hidden from human sight;
They lie abreast of Carnsore Head, and west of Tuskar Light.

Men, women and children were filled with great surprise
A heart like flint it would relent to hear their dismal cries.
We hoist a light from our mast-head before it was daylight
And to our joy and great surprise a schooner hove in sight.

Captain Walsh gave orders unto his seamen brave,
The women and the children to strive first for to save
With that the Glasgow gave a lurch, and none could her prevent,
And five-and-twenty fine young men down to the bottom went.

Long life to Captain Walsh and to his seamen brave,
But for his assistance we'd have met a watery grave.
He landed us in Wexford town where we were treated kind.
In time of need indeed 'twas there some warm friends we did find.

In these four months four vessels wrecked upon the watery main:
The *Glasgow* and the *Mexico*, the *Bristol* and the *Jane*.
And nearly a thousand passengers lie asleep in watery graves
Men who thought to settle in land that never sheltered slaves.

35. Sweet Cootehill Town

Now fare you well, sweet Coote-hill town, the place where I was born and bred. Thro'
sha-dy groves and flow-ery hills, my youth-ful fan-cy did ser-en-ade. But
now I'm bound for A-mer-i-kay, a count-ry that I nev-er saw; Those
pleas-ant scenes I'll al-ways mind, when I am rov-ing far a-wa'.

The pleasant hills near Cootehill town where I have spent my youthful days.
Both day and night I took delight in dancing and in harmless plays.
But while I rove from town to town, fond mem'ry in my mind will stay
Of those pleasant, happy youthful hours that now are spent and pass'd away.

I hope kind fate will reinstate – that fortune's face will on me smile.
And safe conduct me home again to my own dear native Irish isle:
When my comrades all and friends likewise will throng around and thus will say:–
'We will sing and play as in days of old: so you're welcome home from far away.'

36. The Streams of Bunclody

Traditional Street Ballad Air: Variant of 'Coolfin Lake'

O was I at the moss-house where the birds do in-crease, At the foot of Mount Leins-ter or some sil-ent place Near the Streams of Bun-clo-dy, where all pleas-ures do meet, And all I'd re-quire is one kiss from you Sweet.

If I was in Bunclody I would think myself at home,
'Tis there I would have a sweetheart, but here I have none.
Drinking strong liquor is the height of my cheer –
Here's a health to Bunclody and the lass I love dear.

The cuckoo is a pretty bird, it sings as it flies,
It brings us good tidings and tells us no lies,
It sucks the young bird's eggs to make its voice clear,
And it never cries, 'cuckoo' till the summer is near.

If I was a clerk and could write a good hand,
I would write to my true love that she might understand,
I am a young fellow that is wounded in love,
That lived by Bunclody, but now must remove.

If I was a lark and had wings, I then could fly,
I would go to yon arbour where my love she does lie,
I'd proceed to yon arbour where my love does lie,
And on her fond bosom contented I would die.

The reason my love slights me, as you may understand,
Because she has a freehold, and I have no land,
She has a great store of riches and a large sum of gold,
And everything fitting a house to uphold.

So adieu, my dear father, adieu, my dear mother,
Farewell to my sister, farewell to my brother;
I'm going to America, my fortune for to try;
When I think upon Bunclody, I'm ready to die!

37. The Loss of the Atlantic Steamship

You feel-ing heart-ed Christ-ians of high and low de-gree, I hope you'll pay at-ten-tion and now list-en un-to me, While I re-late the aw-ful fate of count-ry-men so brave, Who were going to seek a for-tune, when they met with a wat-ery grave.

The *Atlantic* was our good ship's name, as you may understand;
With sixty of a gallant crew, most nobly she was manned.
Besides nine hundred passengers with hearts both light and gay
Who little thought 'twould be their fate to sleep within the sea.

'Twas from the docks of Liverpool our gallant ship set sail,
'Twas on the sixth of April, with a sweet and pleasant gale.
She had some hundred Irishmen, who on her deck did flock,
And they gave three cheers for Ireland, as she moved out from the dock.

For eleven days she ploughed the seas, and all things went on well,
And before that sad twelfth morning what a dismal tale to tell —
We steered our course for Halifax, till just at two o'clcok,
It was by a false ill-fated light our good ship struck the rock.

The night was dark and gloomy, and the seas rolled mountains high;
Our captain should have known right well the danger it was nigh.
He cared not for our safety as you may plainly see;
He went to bed and left the ship to prove our destiny.

And in a short time after, both passengers and crew,
All rushed on deck and screamed for help, not knowing what to do.
Now wasn't that an awful shock, that night and they in bed,
When our gallant ship she struck a rock at a place called Meagher's Head.

Oh! had they landed in New York, their friends would happy be;
But alas, these sons of Erin sleep in the briny sea.
Our steamboat, the *Atlantic,* she sank to rise no more,
And many an aching heart is left around green Erin's shore.

38. The Emigrant's Voyage to America

On the twen-ty sec-ond day of march eight-een and nine-ty-four

young a-spir-ing Ir-ish-man sailed for the Yank-ee Shore On

leav-ing Queens-town quay in Cork, on that ev-ent-ful day These

were his words, the part-ing words that lone-ly youth did say

Chorus

Good-bye Er-in's love-ly isle that we may ne'er see more

long fare-well to all my friends that're on the Sham-rock Shore I'm

bound to cross the rag-ing waves, to pros-per if I can With

pros-pects bright be-fore me in the land of Un-cle Sam.

When the tender steamed out from the quay, the shouts and wails arose
On every side I heard those cries, great sorrows to disclose
That monarch of the raging sea lay still beneath my view
That *Teutonic* that no one e'er fear, that never steamed untrue.

Her passengers been got on board, her bells did loudly sound,
Her course then quickly she reversed – we soon were westward bound
And steaming round off Kerry's coast we all gave many a wail
As we took one look, one parting glimpse of lovely Inisfail.

56

When we had sailed two thousand miles across that trackless trail
We spied two gorgeous icebergs and they floating on the main
That morning fair, the sky being clear, on deck we all did run
To view those crystal monsters and they dazzling in the sun.

On Ellis Island we did land, after crossing o'er the seas;
The Stars and Stripes there proudly waved and fluttered in the breeze.
How proud our hearts would beat that day if o'er us could be seen
That ancient flag our own dear flag, the lovely flag of green.

39. Captain Thompson

My mind being much in-clined to cross the rag-ing main, I left my ten-der par-ents in sor-row grief and pain. On board the Fame we thus be-came all pas-sen-gers to be, A-long with Cap-tain Thomp-son to the land of lib-er-tie.

As we were safely sailing to a place called Newfoundland,
The wind arose ahead of us, and our ship was at a stand:
'All hands aloft,' – bold Thompson cries – 'or we'll be cast away;
All firmly stand or we ne'er shall land in the North of Amerikay!'

A mount of ice came moving down anear our gallant main,
But the Lord of mercy He was kind and our lives He did maintain.
Our gallant sailors hauled about and so our ship did save,
Or we were doomed to be entombed in a doleful watery grave.

When we were fairly landed our faint hearts did renew;
But how could I sleep easy, dear Erin, far from you.
I hope the time will come again when our comrades all we'll see,
And once more we'll live together in love and unitie.

40. Herring the King

Words: Traditional
Air: An Bruach 'na Carraige Baine (The Brink of the White Rocks)

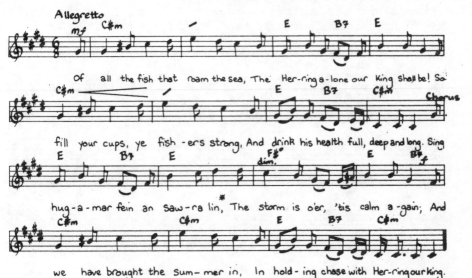

Of all the fish that roam the sea, The Her-ring a-lone our King shall be! So fill your cups, ye fish-ers strong, And drink his health full, deep and long. Sing hug-a-mar fein an saw-ra lin,* The storm is o'er, 'tis calm a-gain; And we have brought the Sum-mer in, In hold-ing chase with Her-ring our king.

I think with me you'll all agree,
We to our King should thankful be.
He clothes us, feeds us, pays the rent,
And cheers us in the time of Lent.

Oh! who would not a fisher be,
And lead a life so wild and free?
Grim care we leave upon the shore
To wait until our voyage is o'er.

Then once more hearken unto me,
The Herring alone our King shall be!
So fill your cups, ye fishers strong,
And drink his health full, deep and long.

* *Thugamar fein an samhrad linn*
(We have brought the summer with us).

59

41. The Kinsale Herring

Traditional: South Coast

There was an old man who came from Kin-sale, Sing a-bor-um fane, sing a-bor-um ling And

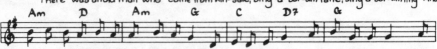

he had a her-ring, a her-ring for sale, Sing a-bor-um fane, sing a-bor-um ling. Sing

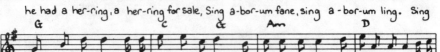

man from Kin-sale, with a her-ring for sale, Sing a-bor-um fane, sing a-bor-um ling. And in-

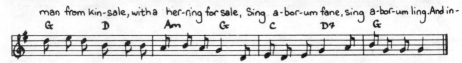

—deed I have more of my her-ring to sing, Sing a-bor-um fane, sing a-bor-um ling.

And what do you think they made of his head? Sing, etc.
The finest griddle that ever baked bred. Sing, etc.
Sing herring, sing head, sing griddle, sing bread. Sing, etc.
And indeed I have more of my herring to sing. Sing, etc.

What do you think they made of his mouth?
The finest kittle that ever did spout,
Sing herring, sing mouth, sing little, sing spout.

And what do you think they made of his back?
A nice little man, his name it was Jack.
Sing herring, sing back, sing man, sing Jack.

And what do you think they made of his belly?
A nice little girl, her name it was Nelly.
Sing herring, sing belly, sing ger-l, sing Nelly.

And what do you think they made of his bones?
The finest hammer that ever broke stones.
Sing herring, sing bones, sing hammer, sing stones.

And what do you think they made of his bottom?
The finest old woman that ever spun cotton.
Sing herring, sing bottom, sing woman, sing cotton.

And what do you think they made of his tail?
The finest ship that ever did sail.
Sing herring, sing tail, sing ship, sing sail,
And I have no more of my herring to sing.

42. The Queen of Connemara

Words: Frank A. Fahy

When she's loaded down with fish,
'Till the water lips the gunwale,
Not a drop she'll take aboard her
That would wash a fly away;
From the fleet she speeds out quickly
Like a greyhound from her kennel,
'Till she lands her silvery store the first
On old Kinvara Quay.
Chorus:

There's a light shines out afar
And it keeps me from dismaying –
When the clouds are ink above us,
And the sea runs white with foam,
In a cot in Connemara
There's a wife and wee ones praying
To the One Who walked the waters once
To bring us safely home.
Chorus:

61

43. The Banks of Newfoundland

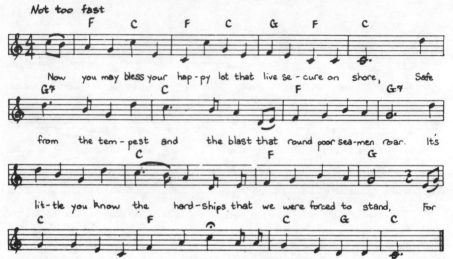

Now you may bless your hap-py lot that live se-cure on shore, Safe
from the tem-pest and the blast that round poor sea-men roar. It's
lit-tle you know the hard-ships that we were forced to stand, For
four-teen days and four-teen nights on the Banks of New-found-land.

Our good ship never crossed before the stormy western waves;
The dashing seas came tossing down and broke her into staves,
She was built of green, unseasoned wood, and could but little stand,
The hurricane that met us on the Banks of Newfoundland.

We had Barney Lynch from Ballynahinch, Tim Sweeny and Mike Moore;
We pawned our clothes in Liverpool in Eighteen forty-four;
We pawned our clothes in Liverpool and sold them out of hand
Nor thought of the cold nor'wester on the Banks of Newfoundland.

The ice fell down in torrents, from the time we left Quebec,
Unless we'd walk within our shoes we'd be frozen on the deck.
We were stout, hardy Irish boys that our good ship did man,
And the captain doubled each man's grub on the Banks of Newfoundland.

The gale it blew from sunset till we sailed three mornings' dawn,
And when she fell to lee-ward two of our masts were gone.
We lashed ourselves to the mizen yards, and 'twas then we verily planned,
To show some signals of distress on the Banks of Newfoundland.

If you were to see us famishing, your heart would feel the pain;
For out of two and twenty, eleven did remain.
Some jumped in earnest in the seas and said they'd swim to land;
But alas, we were one hundred leagues from the shore of Newfoundland.

We fasted, boys, for five long days, our provisions being all out;
And on the morning of the sixth we cast the lot about.
The lot fell on the captain's son, but thinking relief at hand,
We spared him for another day on the Banks of Newfoundland.

No sail appeared next morning and the captain's son prepared;
We gave him another hour, for to offer up a prayer,
When boundless Providence proved kind, and from blood saved every man;
An English vessel hove in sight on the Banks of Newfoundland.

When we were taken from the wreck, we were more like ghosts than men;
They fed us and they clothed us, and brought us home again.
And our dear friends, that lost their lives, they ne'er saw the Irish land,
For the raging waves roll o'er their graves on the Banks of Newfoundland.

'Twas on the seventh of January, this disaster it took place;
It would rend the heart of adamant, and of those that hear their fate.
For eleven of our gallant boys those hardships could not stand.
May Our Saviour's mercy reach their souls on the Banks of Newfoundland.

44. The Faythe Fishing Fleet

Attributed to Twomey, Blackwater

The Faythe fish-ing craft on the twelfth of Nov-em-ber Their fin-ny thread mesh-es they spread o'er the deep: Ser - ene were the heav-ens, full well I re-mem-ber, The wind in its cav-ern was bur-ied in sleep. Tran - quil the sea was, no great - er our pleas-ure, Save that of rel-i-gion, blest heav-en-ly treas-ure. Ere the mid-time of night loud-ly roared be-yond meas-ure A tem-pest whose viol-ence caused ma-ny to weep.

A red bolt of Jove o'er our heads burst asunder;
Heaven's bosom seemed open; astounded each crew;
The sulphuring crash filled all hearts with wonder;
A storm showing presage each pilot well knew.
The dark'ning clouds southward came heavily lowering;
The cataracts of heaven in torrents came pouring;
The winds o'er the ocean were dreadfully roaring;
To shun them, each coast-boat to shore quickly flew.

Not so with us Wexfordmen, awful the dangers,
For we had to brave out the shoals of the Bar,
Unwilling to land on the strand, being all strangers
Though homeward to guide us shone no moon or star.
But the tragical muse fomented devotion;
'Midst the loud crashing elements' dreadful commotion,
These two Wexford skiffs braved the horrors of ocean
Till the twilight of morning arose from afar.

By morning the fierce howling storm it grew stronger,
Our master cried: 'Boys, let us push to the shore:
At anchor our light skiffs can ride here no longer.'
So with fore-sail unfurled we scudded before.
But the life-streaming blood did soon cease its flowing
Of five loving husbands in the prime of life glowing;
By a huge mountain wave, was their skiff overthrown,
And it sank them alas, for to rise never more.

Our fates hadn't yet been commissioned by heaven.
Our threads of existence to sever in twain;
By that same tyrant wave was our skiff on shore driven;
Half drowned we escaped from the terrific main.
What shafts of affliction were our bosoms stinging,
In viewing our friends to their shattered skiff clinging,
A big breaker came, dire death with it bringing,
And sank them, alas, in the watery main.

No more did I see them arise o'er the billows;
Brave Roche, ere going down, waved a long, long adieu.
In death I saw victims, they're numbered poor fellows;
To Heaven's tribunal their spirits quick flew.
Man's life's but a span, how entrancing and fleeting;
What pen can express that sad sorrowful greeting,
Or what pencil portray the dark scene of the meeting,
When home to their families, their bodies were drew.

I'll now name the crew that nigh Curracloe perished;
They have left their poor families, I sadly deplore
There's Rickards, commander, whom fond parents cherished,
A man who was expert at helm or oar.
Although he was fishing, he could have been guiding,
A proud, stately barque, o'er the green billows riding,
In an all-seeing God, with experience confiding
For long he had practised the nautical lore.

There was Roche, who, from childhood the seas had been roaming;
Then Clarke, Brien and Campbell, alas they're no more.
Their bodies were found when the storm ceased foaming,
Thrown up on the breakers on Blackwater's shore.
They are gone, – but pray heaven – youthful and hoary,
They may view all their friends in eternal glory;
They are laid with their forefathers, famous in story,
From all earthly care in a cold silent tomb.

They are gone; but enough from your slumbers awaken,
You minstrels of Erin, now chant their sad doom.
Like five sturdy oaks by the rude storm shaken,
Cut down 'neath the blast in perfection's full bloom.
Faythemen! when over your heads you see pending
A storm, with the elements do not be contending
To the shore with the coast-boats do you be quick tending,
And think of the Faythemen that are now in the tomb.

45. The Arranmore Boat Song

Words: Alfred P. Graves (from the Irish)   Air: Arran traditional

With swell-ing sail, a - way! a - way! Our bark goes bound-ing o'er the bay! Fare-well, fare-well, old Ar - ran-more! She curt-seys, curt-seys to the shore. Fare-well, fond wives and child-ren dear! From ev-'ry ill Heav'n keep you clear; Till through the surge we stag-ger back, As full of fish as we can pack.

For when we've sowed and gardened here,
Far off to other fields we'll steer;
Our farm upon the distant deep
Where all at once you till and reap.

There, there the reeling ridge we plough,
Our coulter keen the cutter's prow;
While fresh and fresh from out the trawl
The fish by hundreds in we haul.

Thou glorious sun, gleam on above
O'er Ara, Ara of our love.
Ye ocean airs, preserve her peace,
Ye night dews, yield her rich increase.

Until, one glitt'ring realm of grain,
She waves her wand'rers home again;
And we come heaping from our hold
A silver crop, beside the gold.

46. The Holy Ground

Words and Music: Welsh traditional

A - dieu my fair young maid - ens, a thous-and times a - dieu, We must bid good-bye to the Ho - ly Ground, the place that we love true; We will sail the salt seas ov - er, and re - turn a-gain for sure.___ To seek the girls that wait for us - In the Ho - ly Ground once more. Fine girl you are, You're the girl I do a - dore,___ And still I live in hope to see, The Ho - ly Ground once more - Fine girl you are.

We're on the Salt Sea sailing and you are safe behind
Fond letters I will write to you, the secrets of my mind,
Fond letters I will write to you, the girl I do adore
And still I live in hope to see the Holy Ground once more.
Fine girl you are, You're the girl I do adore, *etc.*

I see a storm arising, I can see it coming soon
For the night is dark and dreary, you can scarcely see the moon
And the good old ship she is tossing about, and her riggings is all tore
But still I live in hope to see the Holy Ground once more.
Fine girl you are, You're the girl I do adore, *etc.*

And now the storm is over and we are safe on shore
And a health we'll drink to the Holy Ground and the girls we do adore.
We will drink strong ale and porter, and make the taprooms roar
And when our money is all spent we will go to sea for more.
Fine girl you are, You're the girl I do adore,
And still I live in hope to see,
The Holy Ground once more – FINE GIRL YOU ARE!

47. Bantry Bay

Words and Music: J. L. Molloy

As I'm sit-ting all a-lone in the gloam - ing, It might have been but yes-ter-day That we watched the fish-er sails all hom - ing, Till the lit-tle her-ring fleet at an-chor lay. Then the fish-er girls with bas-kets a-swing - ing, Came run-ning down the old stone way. Ev-ery las-sie to her sail-or lad was sing - ing A wel-come back to Ban-try Bay.

Then we heard the pipers sweet note tuning,
And all the lassies turned to hear:
As they mingled with a soft voice crooning,
Till the music floated down the wooden pier,
'Save you kindly Colleens all!' said the piper,
'Hands across the trip while I play.'
And a tender sound of song and merry dancing,
Stole softly over Bantry Bay.

As I'm sit-ting all a-lone in the gloam - ing The shad-ows of the past draw near. And I see the lov-ing fa-ces round me That used to glad the old brown pier. Some are gone up-on their last loved hom - ing, Some are left but they are old and gray. And we're

68

waiting for the tide in the gloam - ing, To sail up-on the Great High - way, To the

land of rest un - end - ing, All peace-ful-ly from Ban-try Bay.

48. Galway Bay

Words: Francis A. Fahy   Air: 'My Irish Molly, O'

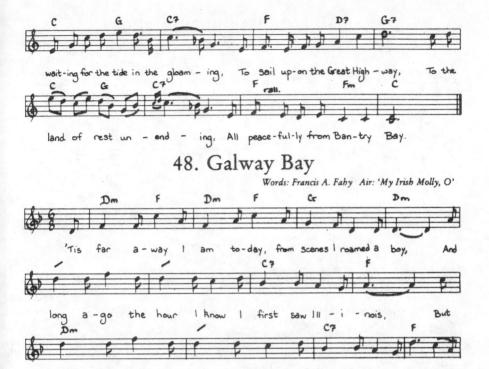

'Tis far a - way I am to-day, from scenes I roamed a boy, And

long a - go the hour I know I first saw Ill - i - nois, But

Time not Tide not wa - ters 'wide, can wean my heart a - way, For

ev - er true it flies to you, My own dear Gal - way Bay.

A prouder man I'd walk the land in health and peace of mind,
If I might toil and strive and moil, nor cast one thought behind:
But what would be the world to me, its rank and rich array,
If memory I lost of thee, my poor old Galway Bay.

Oh, grey and bleak, by shore and creek, the rugged rocks abound,
But sweeter green the grass between than grows on Irish ground,
So friendship fond, all wealth beyond, and love that lives alway,
Bless each poor home beside your foam, my dear old Galway Bay.

Had I youth's blood and hopeful mood and heart of fire once more,
For all the gold the earth might hold I'd never quit your shore;
I'd live content whate'er God sent, with neighbours old and grey,
And lay my bones 'neath churchyard stones beside you, Galway Bay.

The blessings of a poor old man be with you night and day,
The blessings of a lonely man whose heart will soon be clay;
'Tis all the Heaven I'd ask of God upon my dying day –
My soul to soar for evermore above you, Galway Bay.

49a. An tAmhráinín Síodraimín

Traditional: Munster

Tá ú - cair - e mor seang cois Bann - dan is long aig - e,

Amh - ráin - ín síod - raim - ín sios - ú - ram só.

Gearr - chaile is caidhp uir - thi 's greim aige ar chúl uir - thi.

Amh - ráin - ín síod - raim - ín sios - ú - ram só.

Curfá

Máir - tín cé mór liom é, trái - líо - ram, trái - léa - ram,

Mal - ai ghá fua - dach le neart gaoi - the, neart gaoi - the,

Port - láir - ge a's cuan - ta, pá - rú - ram pré - dil - í,

Amh - ráin - ín síod - raim - ín sios - ú - ram só.

Go baile Chionn tSáile chuaigh Máirtín ag píobaireacht;
 Amhráinín síodraimín siosúrám só.
Bhailigh bean agus fiche ar mire 'na thimpeall ann.
 Amhráinín síodraimín siosúram só.

Lean Malaí so mbád é, a's a máthair ghá tionlacan;
Amhráinín síodraimín siosúram só.
Ba ghairid na dhéaidh go raibh Máirtín ar crúca acu.
Amhráinín síodraimín siosúram só.

Tá úcaire mór seang cois Banndan is cúram air;
Amhráinín síodraimín siosúram só.
Beirt bhan sa tinteán a's cliabhán sa gclúid aige.
Amhráinín síodraimín siosúram só.

49b. A Sweet Little Song

Words: James N. Healy   Air: An tAmhráinín Síodraimín

Oh! a tall gangling lad had a boat on the Bandon,
  It's a sweet little song I have here for you now.
And a girl lived near by that he'd put a stray hand on,
  Oh! a sweet little song I have here for you now.

Chorus: 'Martin, come on will you court with me, court with me.'
Molly goes on with her squeezin' him, teasin' him;
Sandycove Harbour, tarum-te-diddle –
It's a sweet little song I have here for you now.

To the town of Kinsale Martin, sporting, is bound him,
  It's a sweet little song I have here for you now.
Before long he had twenty-two women around him,
  Oh! a sweet little song I have here for you now.

Chorus: 'Martin, come on will you court with me, court with me.'
Hear them go on with their squeezin' him, teasin' him;
Sandycove Harbour, tarum-te-diddle –
It's a sweet little song I have here for you now.

But Molly arrived in a boat with her mother,
  It's a sweet little song I have here for you now.
And Martin was hooked, just like many another,
  Oh! a sweet little song I have here for you now.

Chorus: 'Martin, come on will you court with me, court with me.'
Molly goes on, with her squeezin' him, teasin' him;
Sandycove Harbour, tarum-te-diddle –
It's a sweet little song I have here for you now.

If that tall gangling fellow from Bandon was able
  There's a sweet little song that he'd sing for you now.
But besides the two women there's the fill of a cradle,
  Oh! a sweet little song I have here for you now.

Chorus: 'Martin, come on will you court with me, court with me.'
Molly has stopped all that squeezin' him, teasin' him;
Sandycove Harbour, tarum-te-diddle – ·
But the divil a sight does it see of him now.

50. The Cruise of the Calabar

Air: 'Limerick is Beautiful'

Mock-serious, with a lilt

Come all ye boys from Er-in's Isle And list-en un-to my song. Its com-posed of fort-y vers-es And it won't de-tain you long. Its all a-bout the hist-o-ry Of one brave young Ir-ish Tar Who sailed as man be-fore the mast A-board of the Cal-a-bar.

The *Calabar* was a clipper ship
Copper fastened both fore and aft
The rudder was away behind
The wheel a great big shaft
With half a gale to swell her sail
She could do one knot an hour
The fastest craft on the Owenacurra
With only one donkey power.

The captain was a strapping youth
His height being four foot two.
His eyes were red, his ears were green
His nose was a Prussian blue.
He wore a leather medal
He won in the Crimāh war
And his wife was cook, pilot and crew
On board the *Calabar*.

As we went down by the Holy Ground
The stormy wind did blow
Our bo'sun slipped on an orange peel
And fell in the hold below.
The captain cried 'A piratical junk,
And on us she do gain
And if ever I go to Spike again,
Be japers, I'll go by train.'

Now when we rounded Roches Point
A very dangerous part
Our ship she struck a knob of coal
Which wasn't marked on the chart
To stop the vessel from sinking
And save our precious lives
We threw the cargo overboard,
Including the captain's wife.

We got out our ammunition to
Meet the treacherous foe
We had boarding pikes and
Cutlasses and a rolling pin also.
'Put on full speed,' the captain said,
'Or we'll be sorely pressed.
But do not shoot the engineer, for
He is doing his best.'

Oh, the heroes fell both thick and fast,
And pints of blood was split;
They were mostly falling before they
Were hit, in case they might be kilt.
And at last the pirate surrendered his ship
The crew being all flat out.
And we found she was a sister ship,
With a cargo of Murphy's stout.

The ship is in Haulbowline now,
And the crew in the county jail;
And I'm the one surviving
Yet, to tell the terrible tale
But if I could get back to ship
I'd be sailing off afar.
Of the whole bloody fleet I'd be
Admiral, in charge of the *Calabar*.

73

51. The Bug-A-Boo

Traditional Air arr. by James N. Healy

Come all ye tender and faint hearted blokes and a welcome warning take from me, Until I narrate the dangers across on the mighty Sea, Sure many is the toil and trouble, me bonny boys that I've been thro' A-ship with the Steward and the Cook, me boys, a-board of the Bug-a-Boo.

When first I saw the nate little craft she was in the Patrick Street Canal,
She looked so neat and trim, boys, forget her shape I never, never shall,
And the captain he wore an old straw hat, knee-breeches and a body coat of blue,
He cut such a elegant figure-head, me lads, to ornament the *Bug-a-Boo*.

We sailed away till the break of day, and the sea ran mountains high,
And the lightning roared and the thunder flashed, and wrenched the dark red sky,
And the second mate he gave orders for us our sail to clew,
And the captain in his cabin was smoking his dudeen, set fire to the *Bug-a-Boo*.

When the captain found out what he had done he loudly for help did shout,
Shure he bawled out thro' the chimney pot for the helmsman to come and put it out,
But the helmsman he was fast asleep, and we our sails did clew,
And the fire got so far in the middle of the Terf, they couldn't save the *Bug-a-Boo*.

We sailed away till the break of day to a latitude of forty-four,
And the poor *Bug-a-Boo* she burnt, me boys, until she couldn't burn anymore,
And the captain he gave orders to lower away the boats and save the crew
And a thousand sods of turf, and eleven million fleas went to blazes in the *Bug-a-Boo*.

52. The Ballad of the Thirteenth Lock

Words: Traditional Air: 'Toor-al-i-ay'

Ev-'ry night of the year a-bout twelve of the clock the
ghosts and the spooks of the dra-per-ty flock Sit
Swing-in' their bod-ies all this and that way And
mourn-ful-ly sing-in' Ri too-ral-i-ay Singin'
toor-al-i-oor-al-i-Too-ral-i-ay sing-in'
too-ral-i oor-al-i, Too-ral-i-ay Sit
Swing-in' their bod-ies both this and that way And
mourn-ful-ly sing-in' Ri'. too-ral-i-ay.

There once was a captain both gallant and bold
And he laughed at the warnings of young and of old
'D'ye think,' he'd remark and most scornfully say,
'That I'd fear a dead ghost singin' Toor-al-i-ay.'

75

Singin' Toor-al-i-oor-al-i, Toor-al-i-ay
Singin' Toor-al-i-oor-al-i, Toor-al-i-ay
And what would you do now, and what would you say
If you met a dead ghost singin' Toor-al-i-ay.

One Saturday night, coming home from Athy
He halted his boat as the lock he passed by
And he jeered as them ghosts sittin' there on the Quay
All mournfully singin', 'Right-Toor-al-i-ay'.

Chorus: Singin' Toor-al-i-oor-al-i, Toor-al-i-ay
Singin' Toor-al-i-oor-al-i, Toor-al-i-ay
And what would you do now, and what would you say
If you met a dead ghost singin' Toor-al-i-ay.

When he reached into Dublin his money was spent
So 'twas in to the manager's office he went
Says the manager nodding, 'A very fined day,'
'H-m, H-m, H-m,' *(Hum)* says the captain, 'Right-Toor-al-i-ay.'

Chorus: Singin' Toor-al-i-oor-al-i, Toor-al-i-ay
Singin' Toor-al-i-oor-al-i, Toor-al-i-ay
For the devil a word me bould captain would say
Barring, 'Toor-al-i, Toor-al-i, Toor-al-i-ay.'

Well, a day or two after he took to his bed
The doctor was sent for but he shook his head.
For there's no such disease in the pharmacal way
That I ever heard tell of as 'Toor-al-i-ay.'

Chorus: Singin' Toor-al-i-oor-al-i, Toor-al-i-ay
Singin' Toor-al-i-oor-al-i, Toor-al-i-ay
For the devil a word me bould captain would say
Barring, 'Toor-al-i, Toor-al-i, Toor-al-i-ay.'

A day or two after me bould captain died
His wife and his childer around him they cried,
And the last words he spoke when they axed him to pray
Was 'Toor-al-i-oor-al-i, Toor-al-i-ay'

Chorus: Singin' Toor-al-i-oor-al-i, Toor-al-i-ay
Singin' Toor-al-i-oor-al-i, Toor-al-i-ay
For the devil a word me bould captain would say
Barring, 'Toor-al-i, Toor-al-i, Toor-al-i-ay.'

53. My Beautiful Shannon

Words: Michael J. Hogan ('Thomond')   Air: Traditional

My beaut-i-ful Shan-non! how bright runs thy stream from the
morn-ing's first smile to the even-ings last beam; Oh!
Sweet are the o-dours that float round thy tide When the
Sum-mer sun glows on thy em-er-ald side!

My beautiful Shannon! how oft have I strayed
On thy wild flowery banks, with my raven-haired maid,
And opened my soul to thy music, that 'rose
On the sweet fairy wind, o'er the summer's repose!

My beautiful Shannon, alone on thy bank
What a banquet of glory my fancy has drank.
There, while thy blue current swept on to the sea,
I stood like a Magian, in converse with thee.

How grandly thy wild hills and dark woodlands frown,
As thy floods glancing splendour between them rolls down,
Majestic and mighty as when from thy side
Great Brian's Kincora looked down on thy side!

'Twas there, by thy stream, dashing brightly along,
My spirit inhaled the wild magic of song;
And there, 'mid the calm floral shades of the grove,
I first drank the golden enchantment of love!

Roll on, kingly river! thou pride of our Isle,
And glorious life-pulse of t e heart of her soil!
The fleets of the world triumphant may ride
On the broad-swelling breast of thy ocean-like tide!

54. The Lake of Coolfin

Words and Air: traditional, arranged by P. W. Joyce

'Twas early one morning young Willy arose, And up to his comrade's bed-chamber he goes. 'Arise, my dear comrade, and let no-one know, 'Tis a fine sunny morning and a-bathing we'll go.'

Young Willy plung'd in, and he swam the lake round;
He swam to an island – 'twas soft marshy ground;
'O comrade, dear comrade, do not venture in,
There is deep and false water in the Lake of Coolfin!'

'Twas early that morning his sister arose;
And up to her mother's bed-chamber she goes:–
'Oh! I dream'd a sad dream about Willy last night;
He was dress'd in a shroud – in a shroud of snow-white!'

'Twas early that morning his mother came there;
She was wringing her hands – she was tearing her hair,
O, woeful the hour your dear Willy plung'd in,
There is deep and false water in the Lake of Coolfin!

And I saw a fair maid standing fast by the shore;
Her face it was pale – she was weeping full sore;
In deep anguish she gaz'd where young Willy plung'd in,
Ah! there's deep and false water in the Lake of Coolfin!

Our full stocklist includes hundreds of Songbooks, Instruction books,
items on the History of Irish Music, Tune Collections
and a special list with audio material.

For our complete catalogue of Irish, Scottish and General Music Books,
Sheetmusic, Cassettes and CDs published and distributed by us,
send your name and address with two international postal reply coupons to :

Ossian Publications Ltd
PO Box 84, Cork, Ireland

O S S I A N